D1530732

On the Map

Creating Modern Maps

Cynthia Kennedy Henzel

ABDO
Publishing Company

Published by ABDO Publishing Company, 8000 West 78th Street, Edina, Minnesota 55439.
Copyright © 2008 by Abdo Consulting Group, Inc. International copyrights reserved in all
countries. No part of this book may be reproduced in any form without written permission from the
publisher. The Checkerboard Library™ is a trademark and logo of ABDO Publishing Company.

Printed in the United States.

Cover Photo: Corbis
Interior Photos: Alamy p. 21; AP Images p. 20; David Rumsey Collection p. 23; Earth
    Observatory/NASA p. 24; iStockphoto p. 10; Library of Congress pp. 5, 6, 7, 9, 12, 13, 15, 17,
    19, 22; National Oceanic and Atmospheric Administration/Department of Commerce p. 11;
    North Wind pp. 14, 16; Lars H. Rohwedder p. 9; USGS p. 27; Visible Earth/NASA p. 25

Series Coordinator: BreAnn Rumsch
Editors: Megan M. Gunderson, BreAnn Rumsch
Art Direction & Cover Design: Neil Klinepier

Library of Congress Cataloging-in-Publication Data

Henzel, Cynthia Kennedy, 1954-
  Creating modern maps / Cynthia Kennedy Henzel.
     p. cm. -- (On the map)
  Includes bibliographical references and index.
  ISBN 978-1-59928-949-6
  1. Cartography--Juvenile literature. I. Title.

GA105.6.H465 2008
526--dc22
                        2007029201

10/08

Contents

Early Mapmaking

In 1507, German **cartographer** Martin Waldseemüller (VAHLT-zay-mul-uhr) made the first world map that included North and South America. However, his map was not very **accurate**. At the time, many places on Earth were still unexplored. For the next 200 years, explorers continued to fill in the world map. This period is called the Age of Exploration.

One famous explorer was England's Sir Francis Drake. In 1577, he began a voyage around the world. Drake explored the western coast of North America. It is still unknown exactly how far north he went. Queen Elizabeth I kept his voyage a secret from other countries. She wanted to claim any newly discovered lands for England.

English explorer Captain James Cook also helped fill in the world map. Cook began exploring the Pacific Ocean in 1768. He mapped New Zealand and the east coast of Australia. He also discovered the Hawaiian Islands, among others.

FUN FACT
America is named after Italian explorer Amerigo Vespucci. In 1499, he suggested that the lands Christopher Columbus discovered in 1492 were part of a new, separate continent.

This map charts the discoveries of many famous explorers. It is one of the first to show the world as two hemispheres.

AYRE   WATER

FIRE

NORTH

NORTH

Baffins Bay

Frisland

Groten land

Dovies straits

THE

Nova Zembla

Iseland

Estetiland

England

SEA

New Brit tayne

Hudsons bay

New found land

Westerne Iles

Ireland

S. Michael

EUROPE

TARTARIA

The Atlan ticke sea

Spayn

AMERICA MEXICANA

New Gra-nada

Westerne Iles

The GOLF

Mexica

Jamaica

P. Rico

S. Bernardo

NORTH SEA

Canary

Iles of C. Verd

AFRICA

ARABIA

The Red sea

Japan Il.

Lau Blada

C. S. Lucar

Los Lardios

S. Corvalos

S. Petro

Nadadores

I. Barbudos

Hispaniola

The Bay of Beghala

S. Matheo

I. Ascension

The Æthiopian Ocean

St. Helena

The INDIAN

Maldiva

Sundæ

The Sea of Lantchidol

The Æquinoctiall   Line   Ocean

ZUR

AMERICA

BRASIL

PERU

GUIANA

Hoorne Flet

Doge Iland

of Peru

The Pacificke Sea

R. de Ianeiro

R. de Plate

I. Martinvaz

Tropick of Capricorn

I. Tristan

C. of good hope

SEA

Romeros

Madagascar

Turse in our age hath theese stroughts beene passed by Englishmen, the first was by Sir Francis Drake An. 1578 the second by M. Thomas Cavendish in the yeare 1586.

The straits of Magellan

The Antartike Circle

MAGALLANICA

SOUTH

THE SOV THERNE VNKNO NE LAND SOVTH

The Antarcticke Circle

This South part of the World containing almost the third part of the Globe is yet vnknowne certayne sea coasts excepted: which rather shew there is a land then discry eyther land, people, or Comodities.

Eclipse of the Sunne

AMERICA   CANADA   BAY OF   FRANCE

As explorers mapped unknown lands, others improved maps of Europe. In about 1533, Dutch mathematician Gemma Frisius created a **survey** method called triangulation.

Triangulation made mapmaking much easier. With this method, surveyors used mathematics to find new **coordinates**. That way, they could take fewer ground measurements. And

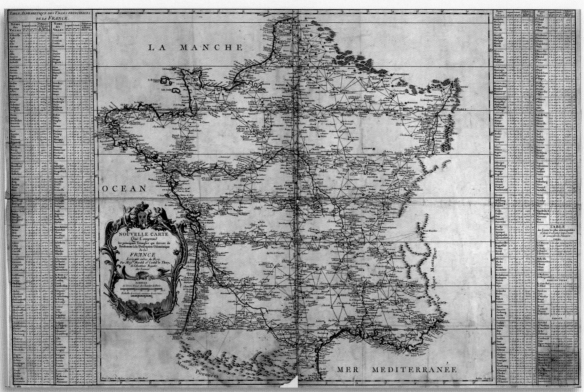

The Cassini map shows how triangulation was used to measure France. Survey markers connect to form triangles that stretch across the countryside.

they could **survey** hard-to-reach places, such as mountainsides.

Triangulation also improved **accuracy**. In 1672, French astronomer Jean-Dominique Cassini and his son Jacques began surveying France with triangulation. They completed their work in 1744. This was the first accurate map of an entire country. Other countries such as Germany, Netherlands, and England soon followed.

In 1747, Jacques's son César-François began working on a more detailed map of France for King Louis XV. The final Cassini map was completed in 1812 by Jacques-Dominique, the great-grandson of Jean-Dominique. It took 140 years and four generations of Cassinis to map all of France!

New Mapping Tools

Scientific discoveries continued to improve mapmaking. However, navigators still had a problem. To plan a route on a map, a navigator drew a straight line between two points. But because the earth is round, ships do not travel along straight lines. Instead, they travel along curves called rhumb lines.

The compass directions for map lines did not account for the earth's curves. So, these readings did not match the rhumb-line compass readings. To fix this problem, mapmaker Gerardus Mercator created a new map **projection** in 1569. On a Mercator projection, rhumb lines appear straight while still reflecting true direction.

After this, navigation continued to improve. In the early 1600s, Italian mathematician Galileo Galilei was the first to use telescopes to map the stars. In 1671, English scientist Sir Isaac Newton made advancements to the telescope. He improved its view by using a curved lens and a mirror to concentrate light.

The Mercator projection shows the round earth on a flat surface. However, scale on this type of map increases with distance from the equator. So, Antarctica looks much larger than it actually is.

Gerardus Mercator

9

AMERICA

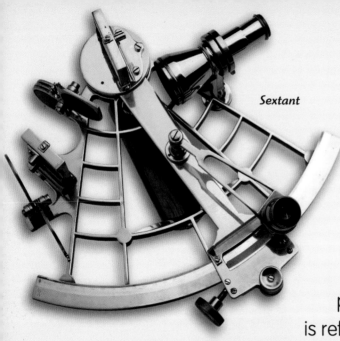
Sextant

Further study of the telescope led to the invention of the sextant in the 1700s. This vital mapping tool used telescope technology to sight the horizon and celestial bodies, such as the sun. With a sextant, one point is sighted while another point is reflected in a mirror.

The distance north or south of the equator is called latitude. It is easy to find with a sextant. Measuring the distance from east to west, or longitude, is more difficult. This is because the earth rotates. Therefore, the angle between the horizon and a celestial body constantly changes. Explorers needed to know both measurements to place a new discovery on a map.

To find longitude, navigators needed a precise clock. English woodworker John Harrison solved

Modern chronometer

this problem in 1735. He invented the chronometer. This device is a clock that reads **accurate** time, even on a bouncing ship. With these new instruments, maps became more exact.

Tricks of the Trade

Determining the location of new discoveries was an important part of exploration. Navigators had to calculate their position in uncharted oceans. Early on, they accomplished this by observing the stars or by measuring the angle between the horizon and the sun. However, these methods could only determine latitude. Navigators also required accurate longitude measurements.

Soon, mapmakers divided the earth into 360 degrees. The earth rotates 15 degrees every hour. So, one hour of time equals 15 degrees of longitude. To find longitude, navigators just needed to know the local time and the time in England.

Navigators could determine the local time on their ship by the position of the sun. But, they also needed a clock set to the time in England. For this, navigators used a chronometer. This reading revealed how far east or west of England they were. After measuring both latitude and longitude, accurate coordinates could finally be charted.

America's First Maps

Mapping played an important role in the exploration of the United States. Maps of new discoveries defined the country's boundaries. They also allowed people to settle new areas.

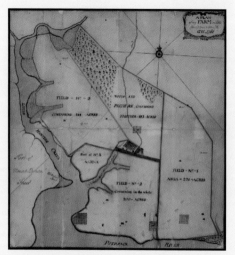

A survey of George Washington's farm

Before becoming America's first president, George Washington worked as a **surveyor**. Washington knew maps could help the nation defend its borders. So in 1777, he appointed Robert Erskine as the first geographer to the Continental army.

The third U.S. president, Thomas Jefferson, bought the Louisiana Territory from France in 1803. This purchase almost doubled the size of America! Soon, Jefferson asked Meriwether Lewis to survey the new land and find a route to the Pacific Ocean. The journey was kept secret

FUN FACT

Three of the four presidents represented on Mount Rushmore worked as surveyors. They are George Washington, Thomas Jefferson, and Abraham Lincoln.

because England still claimed western land discovered by Sir Francis Drake.

Lewis asked William Clark to help lead the expedition and map their route. From 1804 to 1806, Lewis and Clark traveled nearly 8,000 miles (13,000 km) up the Missouri River and across the West. They took **accurate** measurements and made many maps.

Lewis and Clark's journey provided the U.S. government with the first accurate maps of land west of the Mississippi River. The explorers also recorded details of plant and animal life and searched for a trade route to the Pacific Ocean.

Mountain men often served as guides to settlers traveling west.

Explorers called mountain men also made trails in the West. One of the most famous mountain men was Jedediah Strong Smith. He explored and mapped the West from 1822 to 1831.

Smith also told people about South Pass. This valley is the easiest way through the Rocky Mountains. Using this route, Smith became the first person to enter California from the east.

At first, few people wanted to head west. Many people believed the western United States was a big desert. However, John Charles Frémont began exploring the area in 1842. He **surveyed** and mapped what would become the Oregon Trail. His maps and reports about the land encouraged settlers to move west.

Soon, a surveyor named George Gibbs combined information from Smith's and Frémont's maps. The Frémont-Gibbs-Smith map turned out to be the best guide to the West for many years.

Frémont's maps allowed people to see what the West was like before they decided to travel there.

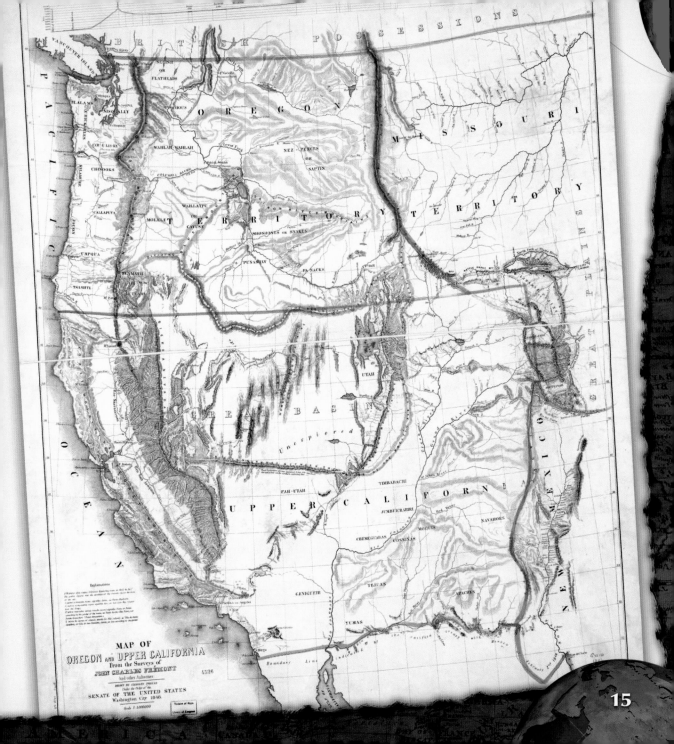

MAP OF
OREGON AND UPPER CALIFORNIA
From the Surveys of
JOHN CHARLES FREMONT
And other Authorities
DRAWN BY CHARLES PREUSS
Under the Order of the
SENATE OF THE UNITED STATES
Washington City 1848.
Scale 1:3000000

15

Defining America

Territorial growth in the United States from 1783 to 1867

Early exploration in America greatly influenced settlement in the West. For example, the discovery of South Pass allowed the United States to challenge the western land claims of Mexico and England.

In 1818, the border between the United States and Canada was set at 49 degrees North latitude from the **plains** to the Rocky Mountains. In 1846, the Oregon Treaty between England and America extended this border all the way to the West Coast.

Then in 1848, gold was discovered in California! Suddenly, everyone wanted to go west. Thousands of Americans traveled west along the Oregon and California trails. The route from Independence, Missouri, toward rich

FUN FACT

Native Americans called the 49th parallel the Medicine Line. American soldiers could not cross the line into Canada. So, the Medicine Line cured the Native Americans of the soldiers' pursuit!

lands of gold was long and perilous. But, maps from the explorers helped the settlers find their way.

That same year, Mexico gave up most of its land claims in the Southwest. Finally in 1853, the U.S. government bought land in Arizona and New Mexico. The Gadsden Purchase completed the outline of the continental United States.

James K. Polk

"54-40 or Fight!"

During the 1800s, the United States and Great Britain each claimed land in Oregon Country. This region included parts of Canada, southern Alaska, and northern California. Great Britain wanted to set the boundary at 42° North latitude. But the United States wanted the boundary set farther north at 54°40' North latitude.

By the 1840s, many Americans believed in the idea of manifest destiny. This idea asserted that all of North America rightfully belonged to the United States. In 1844, James K. Polk ran a successful presidential campaign with the slogan, "Fifty-four Forty or Fight!" This phrase meant that the United States should be prepared to fight Great Britain in order to gain the Oregon Country.

After becoming president, Polk negotiated the Oregon Treaty of 1846. As a result, the 49th parallel became the official boundary between the United States and Canada. This line of latitude continues to serve as the border today.

Printing Techniques

Exploration provided information to make maps and increased demand for them. But, maps were still not easy to obtain. Until the 1400s, most maps were drawn by hand on thin leather called vellum. Since it took a long time to make these maps, they were rare and valuable.

The first printed maps were made with wooden blocks. The block was carved to make a stamp called a woodcut. The woodcut was dipped in ink and stamped onto vellum or paper. In 1482, German printer Lienhart Holle created a book of maps. He used woodcuts to print maps by Ptolemy (TAHL-uh-mee), an ancient Egyptian mapmaker.

Still, woodcut maps had drawbacks. It was difficult to make fine lines, and the blocks wore out quickly. Eventually, printers found that copper plates worked better. First, maps were scratched onto the surface. Then, the grooves were filled with ink and the plate was pressed onto paper. In 1570, geographer Abraham Ortelius used copper plates to create the first modern world **atlas**.

Abraham Ortelius's world atlas reveals many of the geographical details found on today's maps.

Cartographers continued to seek improved methods for mapmaking. In 1798, a printer named Aloys Senefelder discovered **lithography**. He used a stone plate treated with chemicals to make a print. Using a flat plate instead of a grooved one resulted in much finer maps. Still, maps were only printed in one color. Painting on other colors by hand was slow and costly.

Then in 1837, printer Godefroy Engelmann tried putting a map through his printer many times. First, he prepared a separate plate for all the elements to be shown in one color. Then he put the map through the press. Each time, a new plate with a different color was used. The final result was a single colorful map!

Some modern-day printers still create images with a lithographic press and traditional limestone blocks.

Today, color **lithography** remains an important printing method.

Over time, technology made maps more affordable. They also became more widely available. Soon, transportation technology began to improve. These advancements were just in time for the next wave of exploration.

How Do They Do That?

Once information is gathered and put together on a map, the map still needs to be reproduced. To do this, map outlines are reproduced on plastic sheets. Each sheet has a coating that cartographers can etch into.

One at a time, each sheet is laid on a table where a soft light shines up through a white plastic surface. This illuminates the lines of the map. A cartographer carefully cuts along the lines and the areas that are to be a certain color on the finished map.

For example, one sheet might have all the lines for rivers, lakes, and other bodies of water that are to be blue. This process is repeated for each color. Then, the plastic sheets are set in a press and a map is printed color by color.

On the Move

Travel was difficult in the 1800s. The trip along the Oregon Trail was about 2,000 miles (3,200 km) long. It could take four months and cost $1,000! Gradually, new inventions made travel easier. The first of these were the railroad and the steam locomotive.

John Thomson made the first American railroad **survey** map in 1809. It showed a tiny railroad in Pennsylvania. In 1869, the first railroad to connect the East and West coasts was completed.

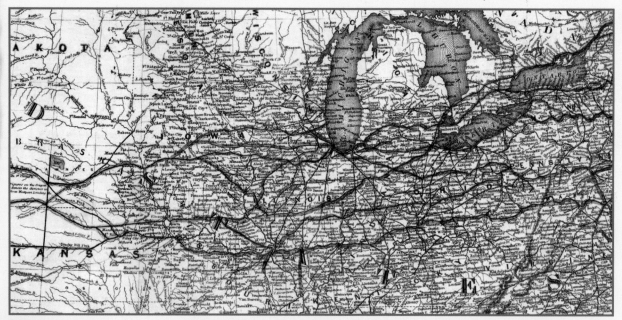

This map of the United States from the 1850s shows the Union Pacific Railroad lines planned between 36 and 47 degrees North latitude.

Much of it followed the Oregon Trail. Suddenly, people could travel across the country in just a week and for a fraction of the cost!

Easier travel made maps more desirable. In 1872, the Rand McNally company began publishing railway guides. It quickly became famous for these guides.

Other groups also began forming. The U.S. Geological **Survey** (USGS) was created in 1879. This is the biggest **civilian** mapping agency in the country. In 1888, the National Geographic Society formed to promote geographic knowledge. It also began publishing beautiful maps for its magazine.

In the 1900s, the automobile became the most widely used form of transportation. Now people could easily explore America on their own time. But, they needed road maps! Rand McNally printed its first road map in 1904. And for many years, oil companies gave away road maps to promote their businesses.

Oil companies stopped giving away free road maps in the 1970s to save money.

SAN FRANCISCO
STREET AND VICINITY MAPS

Sidewalk Flower Stand

CHEVRON SUPREME GASOLINE

HEAVY DUTY RPM MOTOR OIL

A New View

New transportation technology did more than increase the need for maps. It also made mapmaking easier and more **accurate**. In 1858, the first aerial photographs were taken from a hot-air balloon. These photographs gave people a new view of the earth.

In the early 1900s, aerial photography developed with the invention of the airplane. During **World War I**, militaries used airplanes to take aerial photographs. This way, enemy territory could be mapped.

Today, **satellites** map the earth in a

This aerial view of Detroit, Michigan, was captured with satellite imaging.

new way. Aerial photographs show the earth as our eyes would see it. But, **satellites** record bands of the **electromagnetic spectrum** that are invisible to our eyes.

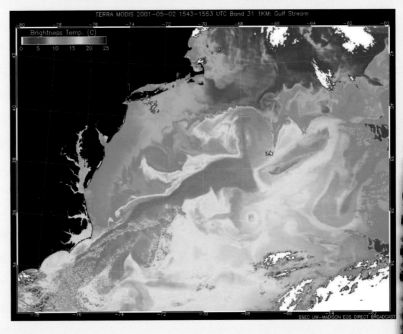

This satellite image shows water temperatures of the Gulf Stream. The water is in color and the land is black.

Satellites that record these energy bands help us map things we normally cannot see. **Infrared** rays determine sea surface temperatures. And, **ultraviolet** rays reveal forest health and underground canals and minerals.

Satellites are useful tools for many jobs. They are used to map large weather systems. And, weather satellites provide continuous information about changes on the ground. This makes it easier to warn people as dangerous situations develop.

GIS Technology

Today, most maps are made with computers. This method is called computer **cartography**. Using computers makes mapping much faster and easier. The modern world has a lot of information to map. For each city, there may be data about transportation, people, buildings, and more.

Luckily, a Geographic Information System (GIS) makes mapping this information much easier. A GIS is a computer system that stores, connects, and displays information about a place. It organizes this information in layers, much like a sandwich. Various combinations of these layers can identify new information and be mapped.

Governments and businesses use GIS technology for planning. It can help solve **complex** problems. A GIS could help identify where to build a new school or a cellular phone tower.

Scientists use GIS technology, too. Information from **satellite** images, animal and plant **surveys**, and historical data is put into a GIS. Sensitive areas can be monitored. And, new areas that need protection can be identified.

For centuries, maps have helped explorers discover new lands. And more recently, they have helped scientists understand and interpret our world. Modern mapping is about more than knowing where things are and how to get from here to there. It is a vital tool for planning our future.

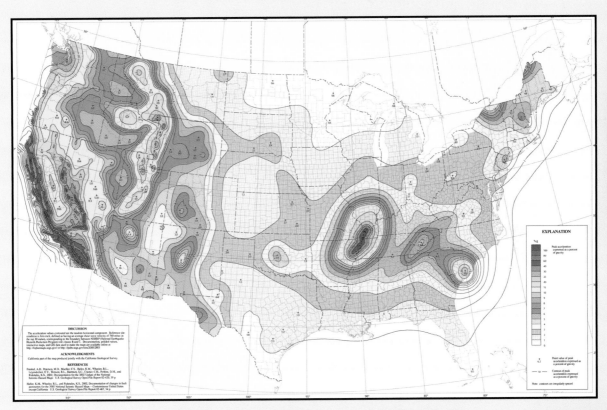

This GIS-made map identifies the areas in the United States that are most likely to experience earthquakes.

Mapping

1507 Martin Waldseemüller printed the first world map that included North and South America.

1533 Gemma Frisius invented the triangulation survey method.

1569 Gerardus Mercator created the Mercator projection.

1570 Abraham Ortelius used copper plates to create the first modern world atlas.

1577 Sir Francis Drake began his voyage around the world.

1672 The Cassini family began surveying France.

1735 John Harrison invented the chronometer.

1768 Captain James Cook began his Pacific explorations.

1777 George Washington appointed Robert Erskine as the first geographer to the Continental army.

1798 Aloys Senefelder discovered lithography.

1803 Thomas Jefferson approved the Louisiana Purchase.

1804 Meriwether Lewis and William Clark began their exploration of the West.

Milestones

1809 The first American railroad survey was conducted.

1818 The boundary between the United States and Canada was established across the plains at the 49th parallel.

1822 Jedediah Strong Smith began exploring the West.

1837 Godefroy Engelmann invented color lithography.

1842 John Charles Frémont began mapping the western United States.

1846 The boundary between the United States and Canada was extended to the West Coast.

1853 The Gadsden Purchase completed the outline of the continental United States.

1858 The first aerial photograph was taken from a hot-air balloon.

1869 The first transcontinental railroad was completed.

1872 Rand McNally printed its first railway guide.

1879 The U.S. Geological Survey was created.

1888 The National Geographic Society formed.

1904 Rand McNally published its first road map.

Glossary

accurate - free of errors.

atlas - a book of maps.

cartographer - a maker of maps or charts.

civilian - of or relating to something nonmilitary.

complex - having many parts, details, ideas, or functions.

coordinate - any of a set of numbers used to locate a point on a line or a surface.

electromagnetic spectrum - the entire range of wavelengths or frequencies of electromagnetic waves. It includes gamma rays, radio waves, and visible light.

infrared - a form of heated energy that resembles visible light but cannot be seen by the human eye.

lithography - the art or the process of printing from a smooth, flat stone or a metal plate on which the picture or design is made with a material that will hold printing ink and the rest of the surface is made ink repellent with water.

plain - a flat or rolling stretch of land without trees.

projection - the representation, upon a flat surface, of all or part of the surface of the earth or another celestial sphere.

satellite - a manufactured object that orbits Earth.

survey - to measure the size, the shape, and the position of an area of land or a feature on that land. A surveyor is a person who surveys.

ultraviolet - a type of light that cannot be seen with the human eye.

World War I - from 1914 to 1918, fought in Europe. Great Britain, France, Russia, the United States, and their allies were on one side. Germany, Austria-Hungary, and their allies were on the other side.

Web Sites

To learn more about cartography, visit ABDO Publishing Company on the World Wide Web at **www.abdopublishing.com**. Web sites about cartography are featured on our Book Links page. These links are routinely monitored and updated to provide the most current information available.

Index